The Parting Glass

A TOAST TO THE TRADITIONAL PUBS OF IRELAND

ERIC ROTH

with Eileen McNamara

STEWART, TABORI & CHANG
New York

To Becky

who believes in making great things possible. She's also more than half Irish, and a very good wife.

Acknowledgments

From the very beginning, this book has gathered momentum, and taken on a life of its own. It has been nurtured by many caring hands. Every single pub owner, employee, and customer we approached was friendly, enthusiastic, and much more helpful than we had any right to expect. To mention just one pub owner by name, Hannah Griffin of Castletownroche has a special place in my heart. With her generosity, she epitomizes the spirit that made this book possible. It is simply the unfailingly good nature of the Irish people we have to be thankful for.

Working with the great writer Eileen McNamara, agents Colleen Mohyde and Frances Kennedy, manager Sabrina Velandry, editors Anne Kostick and Dervla Kelly, designer Pamela Geismar, illustrator Tony Morse, and pubquest traveler and assistant photographer Russ Mezikofsky has been pure joy. I wish it would never end, but I'm glad the book is done and in your hands.

It is my hope this book may be as timeless as the pubs themselves, and be a legitimate document of this noble, humble piece of humanity, culture, and history.

Published in 2006 by
Stewart, Tabori & Chang
115 West 18th Street
New York, NY 10011
www.abramsbooks.com

LIBRARY OF CONGRESS CATALOGING-IN-PUBLICATION DATA
Roth, Eric.
    The parting glass : a toast to the traditional pubs of Ireland / Eric Roth with Eileen McNamara.
        p.cm.
    ISBN 1-58479-438-0
    1. Bars (Drinking establishments)--Ireland--Directories. I. McNamara, Eileen. II. Title.
TX950.53.R51 2006
    647.95417--dc22   2005044111

Edited by Anne Kostick and Dervla Kelly
Production by Kim Tyner
Designed by Pamela Geismar
The text of this book was composed in Joanna and Bureau Grotesque.

Page 1: Six-year-old Niamh Cannon in front of her uncle's pub, Blouser's, Westport.
Page 2: The Palace Bar, Dublin.

PRINTED IN SINGAPORE

10 9 8 7 6 5 4 3 2 1

First Printing

Stewart, Tabori & Chang is a subsidiary of La Martinière Groupe

It all started as it should, over a pint of Guinness.

Our first, long awaited trip to Ireland, and there we were, drinking in the warmth of Dublin. As Becky and I chatted, we looked around us, glancing at the bar, then over to the snug, at all the pictures on the walls, the rows of bottles, tile floor, and the old tin ceiling.

"This pub is so beautiful," she paused, "in a real sort of way."

"Oh yeah ... Wow, would I love to photograph this place." I kept looking around us. "There's so much life to it." Suddenly, excitement welled up inside me. In that moment, I felt sure something important was happening.

Thinking all night and the next day about THE IDEA, I finally headed for the nearest bookstore. They had no books about pubs. Then to another bookstore ... still not a book about pubs. Then the ultimate test, a search at an Internet cafe, and the verification: no book about Irish pubs! I couldn't believe it.

To me, pubs are the perfect photographic subject. They are rich, deep, and lively; open to the public, yet personal. They wear their past like a costume on stage. With atmosphere, stories, music, and laughter; they welcome, relax, entertain, and provide a place to reflect. As a visitor to Ireland, maybe I can be more appreciative than the locals, who would take their pubs for granted. We Americans long for the roots, connections, and a time and place to meet friends. That's what the Irish find at their neighborhood pub. I have fallen in love with Irish pubs, and after a lifetime of McDonald's, shopping malls, and all the plastic outposts of corporate America, I wish there was a pub in my town. Pubs aren't franchised and plunked down, but are a real part of people's lives. They are a public place that feels like home. They're meant to be there.

I was resolved to photograph the "real pubs" of Ireland. Tourist guidebooks say there are more than 10,000 Irish pubs, so I knew we would be doing a ruthless amount of editing to create this book. We were to become pub aficionados, passing through city, town, and village; signaling "thumbs up" or more likely, "thumbs down." Quick glances in countless pub windows revealed whether the atmosphere was authentic, full of traditional pub character, and with the unique personality of a "real pub." Many large towns and even major cities have hundreds of charming pubs, but a precious few that were right for this book. Having been modernized, most would have photographed with the mundane feel of a "bar." The few special pubs that got the nod were usually pre-1950 and unchanged since then, family owned, and a colorful cog of the community.

Our pub-shooting trips were liberating. A few Aer Lingus tickets and a rental car, and we were off. We made no hotel reservations or calls ahead; in fact the usual tourist arrangements would have only been a nuisance. The pubs dictated our itinerary. Driving thousands of miles on country roads, we would find an occasional good pub, introduce ourselves to the owner as a photographer and a writer from Boston, and be received by open arms every single time. Many of the proprietors had more relatives in Boston than in Ireland! After each wonderful photo and chat session, we bid farewell, and were off with new leads for the next stop on our fabulous "pubquest."

Key to pubs

	PUB NAME	TOWN	COUNTY
1	Davy Byrne's	Dublin City	Dublin
2	John Kehoe	Dublin City	Dublin
3	John Mulligan	Dublin City	Dublin
4	Kavanagh's	Dublin City	Dublin
5	McDaid's	Dublin City	Dublin
6	The Brazen Head	Dublin City	Dublin
7	The Long Hall	Dublin City	Dublin
8	The Palace Bar	Dublin City	Dublin
9	The Stag's Head	Dublin City	Dublin
10	The Swan Bar	Dublin City	Dublin
11	The Temple Bar	Dublin City	Dublin
12	The Quays Bar	Dublin City	Dublin
13	The Waxie Dargle	Dublin City	Dublin
14	Toner's	Dublin City	Dublin
15	Morrissey's	Abbeyleix	Laois
16	The Bridge Bar	Arklow	Wicklow
17	Lenahan's	Kilkenny	Kilkenny
18	McCarthy's Bar Hotel	Fethard	Tipperary
19	Griffin's Pub	Castletownroche	Cork
20	H. M. Grindel	Ballyhooly	Cork
21	The Castle Inn	Cork City	Cork
22	The Lobby Pub	Cork City	Cork
23	O'Neill's	Butlerstown	Cork
24	De Barra	Clonakilty	Cork
25	Ma Murphy's	Bantry	Cork
26	MacCarthy's Bar	Castletownbere	Cork
27	The Dingle Pub	Dingle	Kerry
28	Dan Foley's Pub	Annascaul	Kerry
29	South Pole Inn	Annascaul	Kerry
30	Teac Sean	Annascaul	Kerry
31	Daly's	Ennistymon	Clare
32	Byrne's	Ennistymon	Clare
33	P. Frawley	Lahinch	Clare
34	M. Green	Kinvara	Galway
35	Tomás Ó Riada	Galway City	Galway
36	An Tuirne	Kilbeggan	Westmeath
37	Sean's Bar	Athlone	Westmeath
38	Campbell's Pub	Liscarney	Mayo
39	Blouser's Pub	Westport	Mayo
40	Leonard's	Lahardaun	Mayo
41	V. J. Doherty	Ballina	Mayo
42	Hargadon Bros.	Sligo Town	Sligo
43	Thomas Connolly's	Sligo Town	Sligo

It is not for the hot whiskey alone

that Johnny McAndrew walks the mile to Leonard's from his small farm on the outskirts of Lahardaun. The grizzled bachelor's ritual stroll is enlivened by the anticipation of a kiss on his weathered cheek from the ponytailed daughter of the pub's proprietor. With Bubbles the sheepdog at her heels, sixteen-year-old Aileen Leonard tends the bar, stocks the grocery, and pumps the petrol on Saturdays to spell her da from the relentless duties that define the life of an Irish publican.

Before Johnny can hoist himself onto his corner stool, Aileen is pouring the steaming whiskey into the glass tumbler he prefers, replenishing the contents without prompting as the morning wears on and the earthen smell from his rubber boots melds with the linseed oil she rubs into the wide pine bar.

Leonard's sits at the edge of this small County Mayo village, in the shadow of Nephin Mountain, hard by the local funeral parlor, conveniently located for the catering of wakes and burials. (J. P. Leonard is also the local undertaker.) With its smooth stone floors, its old brass taps, and its glass-front cupboards stocked with crackers and tea and raspberry creams, Leonard's typifies an iconic Irish institution fast fading into history; the traditional pub. It is part grocery, part hardware store, part community center and, yes, part drinking establishment. Here, an angler after wild brown trout in Lough Conn can buy his bait, a farmer can replace his broken pitchfork, and Johnny McAndrew can pass a Saturday morning in company more congenial than that of his cows.

The country pub and its more ornate city cousin are falling victim to the roaring Irish economy that threatens old habits even as it produces new jobs.

Prosperity has not made the Irish drink less: One study, in fact, suggests that consumption of alcohol increased by forty-one percent in the last decade of the twentieth century despite the abstemious, who still take "The Pledge" to never let alcohol pass their lips. But a younger, more cosmopolitan workforce in a country of 3.9 million people has fueled demands for a livelier bar scene. A rush to renovate and expand has swept through tiny rural pubs and historic Dublin taverns alike, stripping away many of the distinguishing features that made them Irish originals. The current trend is toward "superpubs," licensed establishments on steroids, designed to accommodate as many as a thousand patrons at a time. Karaoke machines, pool tables, and large-screen TVs are fast replacing the humble hearths, the cracked leather stools, and the sawdust-covered floors that have long been the natural background to the spontaneous conversation, traditional music, and fierce political debate for which this island nation is known. (A monument in the village of Lahardaun memorializes Father James Conroy, a parish priest who was hanged in nearby Castlebar for aiding the French in 1798.)

LEONARD'S
Lahardaun, County Mayo

Following spread: Aileen Leonard cuddles Bubbles while sharing a laugh with Johnny McAndrew.

Ironically, even as so many of the originals disappear,

the universal appeal of the Irish pub has created a bizarre export business. Two companies sprang up in Ireland in the 1990s to sell prefabricated Irish pubs around the world. Now, in Atlanta or Houston, Sydney or Singapore, you will be able to slake a thirst with a pint of Guinness to the recorded sounds of Celtic fiddles and tin whistles. In a lucrative bit of synergy, Guinness, the Dublin brewery that has been bottling porter since 1759, is affiliated with The Irish Pub Company. Both IPCo and the Irish Pub Design and Development Company are marketing "the pub concept" to the world, even as the real article vanishes at home. By 2004, The Irish Pub Company had built more than four hundred pubs in forty countries, including the Matsumoto Irish Pub in Japan and Shanghai O'Malley's in China. The Irish Pub Design and Development Company lets customers select which "authentic" version of a faux pub they prefer: the cottage pub, the old brewery house, the shop pub, the Gaelic pub, the Victorian pub, or the contemporary pub.

Change does not come easily to Ireland, though, so there is some spirited resistance to the new, homogenized pub scene. In Dublin, whose gaslit pubs were immortalized by James Joyce in *Ulysses*, and in small towns, whose entire populations could not fill a superpub, there are stubborn holdouts who prefer preservation to renovation. In city and countryside alike, there are still places where the pubs look and feel as they did a hundred years ago, when the publican's great-grandfather was probably the man pulling the pints.

Of an estimated eleven thousand pubs in the Republic of Ireland, eighty-eight percent are family-owned, the surnames spelled out in colorful block letters above the front door. First licensed in 1635, Irish pubs now answer to the more than eighty laws that regulate a drinking trade that began when ancient agrarian societies first figured out how to ferment wild barley. In Ireland, historians trace ale-brewing back more than eight hundred years, to St. Francis Abbey, the ruins of which can still be seen on the property of Smithwick's brewery in Kilkenny.

There are some notable regional exceptions to the family pub tradition. In County Cork, for instance, local breweries followed the English model: most of the pubs in Cork City were opened by the breweries in order to promote their brands. As a result, you are more likely to see a sign for Cork-brewed Murphy's in a local pub window than one for Dublin-brewed Guinness.

Whether they sell burial shrouds or bicycles along with their beer, whether a brewery or the barman owns them, traditional pubs remain as much a fixture of Irish life as the parish church. Metal kegs have replaced the wooden casks that once were suspended above the bar. Women now drink alongside the men. And a bite to eat or a glass of wine can now be had in addition to a pint of lager. But the ambiance of a traditional Irish pub, the warmth that embraces a patron upon entry, is undiminished by time. The challenge facing the Irish pub at the start of the twenty-first century is how to meet the future without forsaking the past.

Price list and old trophies in window of Teac Sean, Annascaul, County Kerry.

PRICE LIST

(Prices include Excise Duty and V.A.T.)

DRAUGHT	QTY	€uro
Stout	Pint	3:20
Ale	568 ml	3:20
Lager		3:40
Cider		4:10.
BOTTLED	**Long Neck**	
	330 ml	
Stout		3:60
Ale		3:60
Lager		3:60
Cider		
SPIRITS	**Half Glass**	
	35.5 ml	3:00
Whiskey		3:00
Vodka		3:00
Gin		
SOFT DRINKS	**Btl.**	
Carbonated beverage	200 ml	1:80
Cola	200 ml	1:80
Mixer	113 ml	1:30
Bottled Water	250 ml	1:85
WINE		
¼ Bottle	187 ml	4:00

Produced & designed by Reflections Designs Tel: 061 469983 OF (087) 8701268

Barr na Sraide

LENEHAN'S
Kilkenny

Above and right: Michael Shea greets local workmen every morning at 7:30 and serves them coffee and a light breakfast. He tends bar at Lenehan's, which calls itself an "old world pub" and hasn't changed since it was built in the 1920s, as can be clearly seen on the following two spreads. Many customers share Michael's love of hurling, the rough and tumble Irish sport, and discuss it daily over their morning coffee or their after-work pint of stout.

When I die I want to decompose in a barrel of porter and be served in all the pubs of Ireland.

James Patrick Donleavy

Above and right: The traditional snug, a cozy enclosure at the front of Lenehan's, has been adapted to modern life and now doubles as an oversize phone booth.

H. M. GRINDEL
Ballyhooly, County Cork

Above and right: H. M. Grindel is a tiny, small-town pub, packing in local folks nightly. The owner, Finbar Grindel, says he has retained the 1940s styling not for nostalgia but for simple economics: he couldn't afford to modernize. Nevertheless, his pub has a beautiful classic bar and an original hand-crafted atmosphere that is familiar and welcoming. Finbar will reminisce while pointing out old photos of his family and other townsfolk. The pub's age makes it feel a bit dark and moody, and soothes those who appreciate a place that will never change. Following spread: Girls with candy pass a pub in Dingle.

The Daly family has not changed a thing

about the storefront pub that bears its name in Ennistymon, a market town on the southern edge of the wild rocky landscape known as The Burren in North Clare. Two miles inland from the Atlantic Ocean, the town is distinguished by the falls of the Cullenagh River, the thunderous roar of which can be heard clearly on a spring afternoon inside Daly's narrow pub on Main Street. The Cascades, as they are known, fall silent in late summer when the river drops low enough for townspeople to walk as easily across the rock ledges as over the ancient arched stone bridge that spans the Cullenagh in the oldest part of town.

It is less the pull of nostalgia than the tyranny of the building inspectors that keeps Daly's so well preserved, says Marie Daly, one of the owner's daughters. She tends the dark wood bar while another daughter runs the bed-and-breakfast upstairs. Marie points to a statue of the Infant of Prague on the cluttered mantelpiece above the coal-burning stove. "I don't think that's moved a bit in twenty years," she says, referring to the time her family has owned the pub and its faded contents, adding, "'fraid to move it, anyway; as soon as you change a thing the inspectors are all over you for permits and such." Besides, the statue "looked just right where it is, so there'd be no need of moving it."

Change for its own sake is a foreign concept in Ireland. In Daly's, mismatched chairs with well-worn cushions line the back wall and surround the stove, as they have for decades. The one recent addition to the décor is a row of Saint Brigid crosses donated by Marie's landlady, which hangs from a rough-hewn ceiling beam. Saint Brigid was said to have plaited rushes into a cross as she prayed over a dying chieftain in medieval Ireland, prompting the pagan king's conversion to Christianity just before his death. Throughout Ireland,

Catholics still plait fresh crosses each year on the saint's feast day, February 1, and hang them over doorways to protect their homes. Marie's landlady had fashioned hers from wood, rope, and even clothespins, one each year, to mark each year of her marriage. But when her husband became a Jehovah's Witness, he insisted that the crosses had to go. They look right at home in a pub, and not without reason. According to legend, Saint Brigid was not only a compassionate abbess, she was a miraculous brewer, as well. One story holds that when the lepers in her care asked for beer and she had none, she blessed their bathwater, turning it into ale.

Unlike Leonard's, Daly's sells neither groceries nor milking buckets. That does not mean the pub is not a multipurpose enterprise, however. Marie's father, Willie Daly, is a publican by trade but a matchmaker by calling. For going on four decades, he has been interviewing prospective spouses and organizing dances, pony jaunts, and picnics to introduce marriage-minded girls to local fellows. Press clippings touting his successes line the whitewashed walls, alongside portraits of some of the icons of Irish literature—William Butler Yeats, Brendan Behan, and James Joyce.

Previous spread: Colorful pub signs are found in every Irish town. Right: An old cast-iron hearth burns peat to warm the guests at Daly's.

Pubs have long played a role in Irish matchmaking.

Wealthy landowners employed matchmakers to ensure that their offspring married within their class; busy farmers used them as a timesaving shortcut to matrimony. Although the practice is disappearing, many pubs still maintain a small room near the entrance for the local matchmaker to conduct his business. The room often doubled as a snug, a place set aside for women to drink without being seen by male patrons, or a passing priest who might be offended by the sight of a female sipping a glass of porter in public. Today, it is more likely to be used for a "hen's party," as bridal showers are commonly known in Ireland.

Every autumn, for more than a century, there has been a Matchmakers Festival in nearby Lisdoonvarna, timed to coincide with the end of the harvesting and haying season. The town, originally selected for the festival because of the mineral springs that attracted so many people to its healing waters, still hosts the annual fair. In the center of Lisdoonvarna is a pub called The Matchmaker.

Willie Daly still relies on old-fashioned instinct to make a match, spurning the computerized questionnaires favored by modern dating services. Young women from as far away as New Hampshire have benefited from his keen eye for a compatible couple, but he has had some notable failures closer to home. Marie is the oldest of Willie's five adult children; none of them is married.

Around the corner from Daly's, time literally has stopped in the small front room of Byrne's. A 150-year-old round-faced mahogany clock on the wall reads 12:19, as it has for decades. Bridget Byrne cannot recall ever having heard it tick. Bridget lives in the back with her elderly mother—over the door to the residence hangs a photograph of the Clare Minor Team

of 1967 that won the Munster basketball title that year with Bridget's two brothers on offense—but the front room has been a pub for more than a century.

Like so many towns in Ireland, Ennistymon's fortunes have mirrored the highs and the lows of Irish history. There are four plaques embedded in walls and bridges around town, marking the spots where Irish insurgents were killed from 1799 to 1920, either in skirmishes with or executions by the British, during the long struggle for Irish independence. The unmarked graves of hundreds of the nearly five thousand people who perished in and around Ennistymon between 1847 and 1851 lie beside the site of a long demolished workhouse that sheltered the starving during the height of the Great Hunger.

The famine that sent so many to their graves sent a million more pouring out of the ports of Ireland, in a wave of emigration that began in 1845 and did not ebb until the "Celtic Tiger," as the roaring Irish economy was known in the 1990s, provided the jobs that could keep its people home. By 1887, when the West Clare Railway literally put Ennistymon on the map, the town and those who had not left for England or America began to prosper. There were fifty-two pubs in Ennistymon when cattle, not cars, clogged the streets. There are fifteen now, no small number for a town with a population of 881 people in 2002. Some, like Byrne's, are open a few hours a day; exactly when is as much a mystery to strangers as it is a certainty to regular patrons.

Bridget used to tend bar all day and into the night, serving drinks and selling fruit and bread behind the counter. But back surgery made long hours standing on the stone floor more difficult for her, and now she opens for only four hours a day.

THE QUAYS BAR
Dublin City

Above and right: Though not old, The Quays Bar in the Temple Bar section of Dublin deserves attention for beautifully reproducing a traditional pub. Boisterous Irish music is heard nightly, amidst carved panel walls and colorful ceramic floors. Following spread: Crowds pack The Quays Bar to enjoy a lively scene.

Left: The Bridge Bar, Arklow, County Wicklow. Above and following spread: The Dingle Pub, Dingle, County Kerry.

DAN FOLEY'S PUB

LIVE
TRADITIONAL
MUSIC

EVERY
THURSDAY
AND
SUNDAY
EVENINGS

GUINNESS
IS GOOD
FOR YOU

ITS AN ILLUSION

DA

The proliferation of supermarkets

in the last quarter of the twentieth century was the death knell for most grocery-pubs across Ireland. In **The Story of The Irish Pub,** Cian Molloy notes that in 1935, **The Licensed Vintner and Grocer** magazine was able to boast that "The Trade sells 95 percent of all foodstuffs and consumable household requisites used in the country." A few decades later, the oranges and tins of tea behind the bar were more likely for show than for sale.

In 1980, the Green family in Kinvara, a fishing village in southern Galway, stopped selling groceries, 120 years after Michael Green opened his pub on the first floor of a three-story building opposite the harbor. The shelves now are stocked with a mind-boggling variety of liquor bottles, but otherwise the place is little changed. Michael's son, Martin, ran the pub after him, necessitating no alteration in the sign that still hangs over the door. Mary Green runs the pub now, moving tables around to accommodate the traditional music sessions that erupt spontaneously year-round but especially in summer, when tourists congregate as the harbor fills with old sailing ships for *Cruinniú na mBád*; an annual festival celebrating Kinvara's maritime history.

Mary lives above the pub and, for the life of her, she cannot imagine living anywhere else. "It suits me," she says of pub-keeping. "It must be in the blood. I love the people and the conversation and, of course, the *craic*," a Gaelic word with no precise English translation. "Fun" is as close an approximation as any to define the expression commonly heard among patrons leaving Green's after an evening of traditional music. "The *craic* was mighty at Mary's tonight!"

Owen Campbell shares Mary Green's satisfaction with life tending bar. Though a more phlegmatic personality than Mary, he too can imagine himself nowhere else than behind the bar that his family has owned for more than a hundred years. Owen learned to pull a pint, slowly, with special care taken to fashion a smooth, clean head, from his grandfather. His granddaughter is learning the same technique from him.

Campbell's sits at the base of Croagh Patrick, one of the holiest pilgrimage sites for Roman Catholics in all of Ireland. At 2,510 feet, the mountain rises in a perfect conical shape above the picturesque seaside town of Westport in County Mayo. Once the site of pagan worship services, it was here, in AD 441, that St. Patrick passed the forty days of Lent in prayer and fasting and from where, according to legend, he banished all the snakes from Ireland.

M. GREEN
Kinvara, County Galway

Previous spread: The colorful Dan Foley's Pub, Annascaul, Dingle Peninsula, County Kerry. Right: Kinvara schoolgirls are happily photographed at a local landmark.

The problem with some people is that when they aren't drunk they're sober.

William Butler Yeats

Left and above: Bottles and glasses cram the shelves of M. Green while t-shirts find a space on the ceiling. Following spread: Owen Campbell tends bar at the pub his family has owned for more than a century at the base of Croagh Patrick in County Mayo.

Every year, a million pilgrims, some of them barefoot

to show repentance for their sins, climb past the white statue of the patron saint of Ireland at the base of Croagh Patrick to the stone church at its summit. As a reward, a breathtaking view of Clew Bay, the Atlantic beyond, and the surrounding countryside greets them.

Campbell's is in a fortuitous location for a pub: if sober-minded penitents righteously reject a pint on the way up, they are likely to crave one when they get back down. The walls of the pub are covered with framed sepia-toned photographs of long-dead men and women in mid-climb. A turf fire burns aromatically in the small grate, casting shadows on the bead board ceiling. The mantelpiece is littered with coins left by drinkers who have come and gone.

A few miles away is Westport proper, one of the few planned towns in Ireland. Laid out by an architect in the eighteenth century, it features both a pretty town square and an elegant tree-lined boulevard known as The Mall that runs along the Carrowbeg River. This Georgian town was the backdrop for *Circle of Friends*, the 1995 Minnie Driver movie based on the novel by Maeve Binchy.

The town is home to scores of pubs, too few of them preserved from the encroachments of the twenty-first century. Just off the square on James Street, though, is Blouser's, established as a grocery-pub in 1893 by Richard Walsh, a civil engineer who lived above the store with his wife, Mary Ann, and their five children. By 1925 his carpenter-son, Thomas, and his daughter-in-law, Bridget, were running the place.

Today the grocery is gone, but the shelves remain, now stocked with bottles of stout. Eamon Canning mans the taps and lives upstairs, managing the pub with the help of his sister, Una Cannon; he has an eye toward owning it himself one day. "Every Irishman's dream, isn't it, to own a pub like this?" Eamon asks, the question clearly rhetorical in his case. His answer to it is obvious in the meticulous care he takes to preserve the place as the quiet refuge it has been for more than a hundred years. So well preserved is Blouser's that Guinness used it as the setting for a recent television commercial. So quiet is it that Una's six-year-old daughter, Niamh, can do the homework, assigned by her Irish-speaking primary school, at the bar without distraction.

The one concession to changing tastes is a converted room one flight up, and a world away from the celery-green colored pub, used for occasional rock concerts for the younger set. "We had a Kurt Cobain tribute band one night that about shook the building off its foundation," Eamon says. "I wouldn't have been in that night," laughs John Moore, a local man who has been warming a certain stool at the corner of the bar several nights a week for most of the last two decades.

BLOUSER'S PUB
Westport, County Mayo

Left: John Moore occupies his favorite corner stool at Blouser's in Westport. Following spread: Eamon Canning lives above Blouser's, where his sister, Una Cannon, helps tend bar and her daughter Niamh often does her homework at one of the pub's long pine tables.

O'NEILL'S
Butlerstown, County Cork

Left and above: Mary O'Neill might preside over the only lilac-colored pub in Ireland, though it is not likely to remain lilac for long. "I get easily bored so I am always changing the paint," she says of the pub where a traditional game of ring toss could be the highlight of an evening's entertainment. The leaded-glass front doors open onto the narrow lane that separates the only pub in Butlerstown, County Cork, from the fields where the town holds its annual pony races.

JOHN KEHOE'S
Dublin City

Left, above, and following spread: Two hundred years old and going strong, John Kehoe's is revered for its unchanged, original atmosphere. It is simply and unassumingly one of the most beautiful pubs in all of Ireland. The snug is lovingly preserved. It hearkens back to the days when women were not allowed in the main areas of Irish pubs, and could only have a drink when it was discreetly passed through an open window into the snug. There the women sat, until the 1960s, when they were accepted into the main pub.

Left: An antique clock, John Kehoe's.
Above: Tom Frawley with his pub of sixty years,
Lahinch, County Clare.

Above: The South Pole Inn of Annascaul on the Dingle peninsula, County Kerry, is dedicated to Tom Crean (1877–1938), a town resident who was a shipmate on the famed Shackleton expedition. Right: The vibrantly colored An Tuirne, Kilbeggan, County Westmeath.

Adrienne MacCarthy never expected to

take over the pub her family has owned for generations in tiny Castletownbere, on the Beara Peninsula in West Cork. She lived in London, liked to travel the world. Why would she want to come back to this small fishing port, to tend bar on a wild, rocky spit of land that juts into the Atlantic?

"I came back and I couldn't leave," she says. Her surname is spelled out in mosaic tiles on the foyer floor of the waterfront pub, next to tins of baking powder and peach preserves stacked alongside boxes of Brillo pads and bottles of Harp on the grocery shelves. Her pugs, Sydney, Bailey, and Alfie, have the run of the place, often taking the afternoon sun in the comfortable snug at the front of the pub. A newspaper clipping on one wall recounts an interview with her late father, Dr. Aiden MacCarthy, a Royal Air Force physician during World War II who survived both Dunkirk and internment by the Japanese in Nagasaki after the United States dropped the atomic bomb in 1945. Adrienne keeps his medals on display, preserved under glass. "He loved this place," she says.

Adrienne's sister, Niki, came for a weekend visit from London a few years back and she never left either. "She spent the first day telling me I was crazy to live out here. Next thing I know she's opening a restaurant four doors down."

Ireland can do that sort of thing to an otherwise sensible person.

MacCarthy's came in for a fair bit of notoriety with the tourists a few years back after British travel writer and humorist, Pete McCarthy, featured a picture of the pub on the cover of his book *McCarthy's Bar*. The book's conceit, that the author never passes a bar with his name on it without stopping, propelled him along the West Coast of Ireland from Cork to Donegal in search of his Irish roots, and his next pint. The author stumbled into Adrienne MacCarthy's pub on her birthday and stayed until four o'clock in the morning, celebrating the event with her family and friends. "It's not so wild in here every night," she laughs. "This is a small town, after all."

Small, but pub-loving, as a government Committee of Inquiry on Intoxicating Liquor found in 1925 when it surveyed the number of licensed establishments in Ireland and discovered that there were twenty-four pubs in Castletownbere—and only forty families. That high number might have come about because the fishing village was once a port for the Royal Navy, Cian Molloy points out in *The Story of The Irish Pub*.

The American television producers who dreamed up *Cheers*, a fictional Boston bar "where everyone knows your name" could have experienced the real thing in any Irish town. Pubs do embrace strangers—tourists often count the memory of a favorite Irish pub the highlight of a trip to the Emerald Isle—but the locals are every publican's livelihood.

MACCARTHY'S BAR
Castletownbere, County Cork

Right: Adrienne MacCarthy proudly displays her late father's World War II medals in her Cork pub. Following spread: Sunlight floods MacCarthy's, creating an inviting and relaxing scene.

No Smoking

Wine comes in at the mouth
And love comes in at the eye;
That's all that we will know for truth
Before we grow old and die.
I lift my glass to my mouth,
I look at you and I sigh.

William Butler Yeats

Left: Part grocery, part pub, MacCarthy's has operated for generations in Castletownbere. Above: Alfie, one of Adrienne's three pugs, enjoys a sunny spot at the front door as he waits for the next patron.

The Castle Inn, the oldest family-run pub in Cork City,

caters to its regulars. Denis and Mary O'Donovan run the place with a part-time assist from their son, Michael, a full-time student of the hospitality trade at the Shannon College of Hotel Management. Instead of stools, the narrow bar features a long wooden bench nearly as worn as the linoleum on the floor. There are a few serviceable tables in the rear, Guinness flags on the wall, and a television always tuned to the horse races or local football or rugby matches—Munster made the rugby semifinals five times in recent years. "The lads come in right after opening at noon," Mary says, referring to men of retirement age. The most voluble on any given day is sure to be Bernie Murphy, a former Cork City councillor whom everyone calls "Doctor" because of the honorary doctor of humanities university degree he picked up on a visit to the United States in his political heyday.

The daytime crowd is older than the one that packs the place after work. In the evening, there are as many women as men, more of them in their twenties than in their sixties. On Saturday night, the snug is usually booked for private parties and patrons are as likely to order vodka as Irish whiskey: since the Irish joined the European Union in 1973, their taste in drink has broadened. In small pubs in the countryside, ordering a glass of Chardonnay is likely to produce a single-serving-sized bottle with a twist-off cap, similar to those favored by the airlines. In Dublin, however, the pubs offer a sizeable and sophisticated wine selection.

Because the wood buildings within the banks of the two rivers that form the city center are packed so tightly together The Castle Inn burns smokeless coal in its small fireplace. "If one were to burn, we'd all burn," says Michael, who hopes to run the pub one day. "This is one of the last old pubs left in Cork. Unless it falls down, we wouldn't be changing it."

THE CASTLE INN
Cork City

Left: Michael O'Donovan pulls the pints in The Castle Inn, the oldest family-run pub in Cork City. His parents, Denis and Mary O'Donovan, own the place. Following page: Bernie Murphy is one of the regulars. A former Cork City Councillor, Murphy is affectionately known as "the doctor," a nod to an honorary degree bestowed on him during a ceremonial visit to the United States in the 1980s.

Right: Street corner pubs reflect in the River Lee, Cork City.

THE LONG HALL
Dublin City

Left, above, and following spread: Ornately decorated in the Victorian style, The Long Hall was named after an English chapel dedicated to Saint George the dragon slayer. This is a dark, rich pub known for a quiet atmosphere. All the stained glass, carved and stenciled woodwork, and brassy ornamentation is cleaned and polished daily.

If he can say as you can
Guinness is good for you
How grand to be a Toucan
Just think what Toucan do

IS FEARRDE TÚ DEOCH

Fáilte go dtí

GUINNESS

Ceol agus Comhrá

GUINNESS FOR STRENGTH

Previous spread: The very tidy Griffin's Pub, Castletownroche, County Cork.

Work is the curse of the drinking class.

Oscar Wilde

GUINNESS
FOR STRENGTH

Right and previous spread: They cannot compete for grandeur with the Victorian taverns in Dublin, but the country pubs of Ireland have a decorative charm distinctly their own. On rural byways it is not uncommon to come upon a roadside pub decked out with gnomes, elves, and vintage brewery signs. The toucan, a favored symbol of Guinness stout, graces everything from weathervanes to clock towers, with such memorable slogans as "Guinness for Strength" and "Black is Beautiful."

Sean's Bar, which advertises itself

as the oldest pub in Ireland, is a happy mix of local patrons and travellers. Renovations at the pub in 1970 uncovered wattle and daub construction—walls made of daubing clay and mud, framed in rough branches—that dates it back to the ninth century. A piece of the exposed wall has been preserved under glass and put on display to give patrons a sense of just how old the place is.

Situated in Athlone, County Westmeath, in the center of Ireland, Sean's sits alongside the Shannon River. Its sloping floors are less a design feature than a sign of age. In the not-unprecedented event of flood, the waters of the Shannon simply roll through the back door and down into the rain-swollen river.

Sean Fitzsimons, for whom a stool is permanently saved at the end of the bar, owns the place, one of eighty-six pubs in Athlone. A brass plaque informs the uninitiated: "This seat reserved for Sean." Old photographs and older artifacts decorate the walls. Above Sean's stool is a clock from the Dublin General Post Office, the site of the doomed 1916 Easter Rising against British rule in Ireland. The rebellion failed, but the high-handed decision by the British to execute the leaders in Kilmainham Jail enraged the populace and elevated the rebels to the status of martyrs, paving the way for future battles and, ultimately, the Irish Free State.

The history attracts tourists, but it is the *craic* that draws the locals in after Sunday Mass to watch young and old shake off the morning sermon and pull stools up to the pub's piano for an impromptu session of traditional music. Sean's has a well-earned reputation for *ceol agus craic*, a social gathering place for traditional Irish music. The scene is especially lively in summer, when the musicians spill out into the beer garden behind the pub to take inspiration from the Shannon flowing nearby.

SEAN'S BAR
Athlone, County Westmeath

Left: The intricately carved door of Sean's reflects the history and age of this Athlone pub. Following spread: Sean's, well known for its music sessions, is a comfortable spot for Barney Dempsey to play the fiddle.

Traditional music is as integral to the Irish pub

scene as porter and whiskey. The indigenous culture never vanished during centuries of British rule, despite the best efforts of Ireland's occupiers to wipe out its language and its music. *Comhaltas Ceoltóirí Éireann*, the National Organization for Irish Traditional Music and Musicians, began the revival in the 1920s, as soon as the country obtained its independence. It has helped to ensure a robust music scene ever since.

It would be hard to find a town in all of Ireland where the sounds of a tin whistle and a bodhran cannot be heard pouring from a pub window on a Saturday night. In De Barra's in the West Cork town of Clonakilty, the photographs on the walls give testa-

ment to the musical legends who have passed through this homey pub on Pearse Street. Whether Paul McCartney, Janis Joplin, Bruce Springsteen, Bob Dylan, Ray Charles, or David Bowie ever played the 200-year-old harp on display near the open fireplace is unknown, but all of them have stopped in at one time or another to catch the *ceol agus craic* in the front room.

The cozy bar suits the informal sessions of local musicians, but when such big names in Irish music as Christy Moore show up to play, as he does three or four times a year, a more formal stage in the back room is pressed into service.

Above and right: Sean's attracts larger crowds on a Sunday where a session of traditional Irish music begins after Mass. The local musicians above are, left to right, Paul O'Shea, Damian Curley, Sinead Curley, Serena Curley, Laura Murray, and Barney Dempsey.

In Bantry, Bill and Pat Leonard serve mussels along

with the music. The Leonards own Ma Murphy's, just up the tidy square from Bantry Bay. During the annual Mussel Fair every summer, they lay out free plates of the freshly-harvested shellfish on the bar for those packing a hunger as well as a thirst.

The pub has been known informally as Ma Murphy's since it opened in 1900, but until the Leonards bought the place in the 1980s, the name above the door was that of Ma's husband, Patrick. Giving Ma her due was Bill's first official act as a new publican. "She was the soul of the pub. She spoiled the people," he says. "Her name needed to be on it."

The pub fell out of the family when Ma and Patrick's daughter had two sons with no interest in running a public house. (One became a priest.) Bill Leonard worked in the pub for six years before he bought it and the town has embraced him and his wife, Pat. "We don't pretend to be locals," says Pat. "You have to have three generations in the graveyard to be a local. We're blow-ins, but we've been welcomed, and the pub is always full."

One of the regulars is a frequent visitor from the United States. A resident of Richmond, Virginia, he gave the Leonards the shadowboxes on the pub wall that display artifacts of the American Civil War. "You won't find these in every Irish pub," says Bill.

The new name and the conversion of the lamps above the bar from gas to electricity is about all that's changed at Murphy's in decades. Bottled beer is stocked in a sixty-year-old Frigidaire with a jerry-rigged handle. The empties are stacked in the old snug. The local supermarket stays open until 10:00 p.m. but, in a pinch, a patron can pick up a box of corn flakes or Jacob's Biscuits at Ma Murphy's.

In winter, the music stays indoors but in fair weather, musicians and smokers share the beer garden behind the pub on the site of an old stable and black-smith shop. Bill, a lifelong smoker, quit because of the smoking ban enacted in 2004. "I just stopped cold," he says. "Everything smells better and, I swear, the music even sounds better."

MA MURPHY'S
Bantry, County Cork

Left and following spread: Bill and Pat Leonard are the proprietors of Ma Murphy's in Bantry. The annual Mussel Fair brings locals and tourists alike to the pub for the pints and the plates of shellfish, fresh from Bantry Bay, that Bill and Pat set out on the old wooden bar. The pub was originally named for Patrick Murphy but Bill changed the name when he bought the place to reflect the well-known fact that it was Ma, not her ne'er-do-well husband, who ran the popular pub for decades.

I have a total irreverence for anything connected with society, except that which makes the road safer, the beer stronger, the old men and women warmer in the winter, and happier in the summer.

Brendan Behan

THE TEMPLE BAR
Dublin City

The Temple Bar is two things. First, it's a friendly, colorful pub founded in 1840. Second, it's the name of a neighborhood in Dublin that is practically cluttered with great Irish music pubs. Above and following spread: By day, The Temple Bar is a local pub with great **craic.** By night, bring on the music! As the official postcard says, "Performance times can be a little erratic; some sessions just start impromptu. No cover charge for these sessions and the musicians do not have to be tipped or bought drinks. Just sit back and enjoy the experience." If you stay in a hotel here, don't bother trying to sleep; exuberant and boisterous youth in the streets below will win out. Though tourists abound, the good-natured spirit and sweet music is purely Irish, and as strong as ever.

> # There are no strangers here, only friends you haven't met yet.
>
> William Butler Yeats

Left: Two locals converse in The Temple Bar.
Following spread: Tomás Ó Riada is nestled in
the heart of Galway City, a hip college town
where music pubs abound.

It is the fishing tackle, not the fiddles,

that lures townspeople and visitors to Vincy Doherty's on Bridge Street in Ballina, the largest town in Mayo. Its front doors bear etched glass inserts that depict an enormous salmon struggling on a line that could have been purchased within. The left half of the pub sells fishing tackle to the thousands of anglers who gravitate to one of the best salmon fisheries in the world. In June and July, says Ned Doherty, the salmon practically jump into the nets of fishermen on the adjacent bridge above the River Moy.

Ned is the fourth generation of his family to tend the bar on the banks of the river. "My two brothers and two sisters had the brains to go off and do something else," he jokes, though he doesn't seem to mean it. The place holds too much family history.

On the wall is a clipping from the *Ballina Herald*, dated April 24, 1913, that announces the sale of the premises to the first of a long line of Dohertys. "C. J. Doherty begs to announce to the public generally that he has taken over the Old Established Premises in Bridge Street, Ballina, formerly known as Egan's, where he intends to carry on and extend the business hitherto connected with this old established House. Nothing but the Best Brands of Liquors, Groceries and Provisions will be stocked and the prices will be most moderate, consistent with the quality of the Goods. The Egg Trade, which has always been a leading feature of the Establishment, will be carried on and extended. [Christmas Day and Good Friday–closed.]"

The habit of conducting two businesses within a single establishment produces some odd sights to the unaccustomed eye. When a funeral procession passes by, Ned Doherty hastily locks the door and pulls the shade down on the bar side of the pub. When the cortege has passed, he unlocks the pub door and lifts the shade. "It is a pub's demonstration of respect for the dead," he explains.

Such quaint and heartfelt displays are seen less often in urban pubs and, by Irish standards, Hargadon Bros. in Sligo Town is an urban pub. It is one of the oldest of the seventy pubs in the hometown of William Butler Yeats, who is buried just north of Sligo at Drumcliff Church. A preserved specimen from a bygone era, Hargadon's is a throwback to a simpler time than the one evident in bustling O'Connell Street outside its front doors.

Hargadon Bros. is a "talking pub." Its dark wooden interior and lack of modern amenities—there is no television set, no pool table, no video games—encourages conversation. There is no decoration beyond the old whiskey jars and wooden casks that line sagging shelves. There is no heat beyond that provided by the iron potbellied stove.

Should she have suffered a sudden thirst, a housewife fifty years ago would have slipped into the stylish snug opposite the grocery counter for a drink. The snug at Hargadon's is unchanged from the days when it was the only place a woman could take a drink outside her home. A door provides privacy from the rest of the pub and small opaque windows that turn on pivots move noiselessly back and forth, allowing the bartender to discreetly slip a drink across the marble countertop into the snug without ever coming face to face with the drinker.

V. J. DOHERTY
Ballina, County Mayo

Right and following page: Fishing photos take the place of the usual brewery signs in V. J. Doherty.

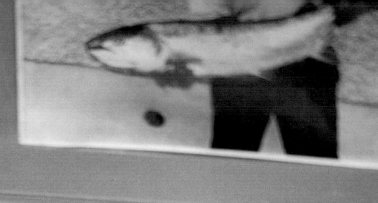

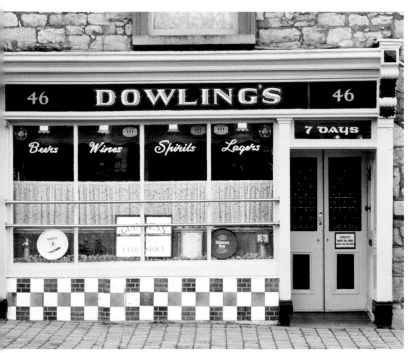

Pubs were men's clubs until the 1960s, when it

became more socially acceptable for women to imbibe in public. It was not until the year 2000, however, that the Equal Status Act made it illegal in Ireland to refuse to serve someone "on the grounds of gender, marital status, family status, sexual orientation, religious belief, age, disability, race or membership of the Traveller Community." (Travellers is the name given in Ireland to the shrinking band of itinerants who wander the countryside and cities.)

The shame attached to women for drinking in public was a modern phenomenon, stoked by the heavy hand of the Roman Catholic Church. In the Middle Ages, it was women who brewed ale for family and for social consumption, and women who distilled whiskey for medicinal uses. Whiskey is called *uisce beatha* in Gaelic, "the water of life." Women were as likely as men to be visitors to the local *shebeen*, the rural drinking dens where *poitin*, the local moonshine, was distributed to revelers from illegal stills.

Hargadon Bros. also boasts a fine collection of pub mirrors, advertising whiskey or cigarettes, although smoking has been prohibited in Irish pubs as a public health measure since March of 2004. A photograph of Hargadon's staff holding a "No Smoking" sign pilfered from The Rosses Lighthouse at the mouth of Sligo Harbor claims a prominent space on the pub's wall. Bartender Oliver Quigley has been surprised at how compliant his clientele, as many as half of them

smokers, has been with the ban. The law, the first of its kind in Europe, was enacted to protect the public from the cancer risks associated with secondhand smoke. Most smokers kick up a fuss about stepping outside at Hargadon's only when especially foul weather means a damp smoke on the wet sidewalk.

Mary O'Neill, proprietress of the only pub in the village of Butlerstown in West Cork, has developed a less than scientific formula for keeping her smokers dry. "Wind and rain from the north, take your cigarette in the front; wind and wet from the south, take your cigarette in the rear," she says. "When it blows in both directions, you're on your own."

Most pub owners, unwilling to pay the heavy fines imposed for defying the law, accepted the change with minor grumbling. Others, claiming a dramatic decline in business the first summer the ban was in effect, defied it. Donall O'Keeffe, chief executive of the Licensed Vintners Association in Dublin, claimed the city's pubs lost fifteen percent of their business in the first three months of the ban. In short-lived acts of defiance, publicans from Dublin to Galway set up smoking areas to keep their tobacco-loving customers happy, but few could afford to sustain their rebellion. Ireland's Office of Tobacco Control reported ninety-seven percent compliance with the law, which polls showed enjoyed broad support among Irish voters.

HARGADON BROS.
Sligo Town

Right and following spread: Hargadon Bros. on O'Connell Street in Sligo is so old that the original wooden grocery counter opposite the mahogany bar tilts perilously toward the stone floor. The shelves are stocked now with empty whiskey jars, stout bottles, and other memorabilia of the pub's storied past.

Left and above: With its potbellied stove and its ban on television and pub games, Hargadon Bros. has a reputation as one of the last "talking pubs" in Ireland, where conversation is more prized than television. In 2005, a new owner lifted a ban on music that had been in place at Hargadon's for more than a century. Talk is still the main diversion, but on Thursday nights conversation now competes with fiddles and tin whistles for the attention of delighted patrons.

It is not the acrid smell of tobacco but the dank

smell of the River Garavogue that permeates Thomas Connolly's, the oldest pub in Sligo Town. The 250-year-old establishment, owned by the Connolly family for 115 of those years, is not afraid to show its age. The paint is peeling; the rope chairs tilt precariously toward the stone floors. At the rear of the pub, the plaster has broken away and you can see the hidden architecture of the place; rows of brick layered on slabs of wood. Still, leather barstools with comfortable curved arms are lined up along the bar. Antique clocks line the shelves, competing for space with more modern timepieces, none set to the same hour. Inside Thomas Connolly's, it could be the nineteenth century as easily as the twenty-first.

THOMAS CONNOLLY'S
Sligo Town

JOHN MULLIGAN'S
Dublin City

Above, right, and following spread: John Mulligan's is, by all accounts, the oldest pub in Dublin. A well-worn antique, it has provided stimulating atmosphere and good company for almost three centuries of Dubliners. In years past, it was a favorite haunt for actors working in the theater next door, who would stop in for shots during intermission. It's still hallowed ground for politicians, journalists, and business people. It doesn't have music sessions, television, or tourist attractions—this is a pure Irish pub.

The sense of timelessness is especially

acute in those Dublin pubs that have not fallen victim to the renovators. Many of the taverns featured in **Historic Pubs of Ireland,** a 2001 travel guide, retain their period exteriors but have been gutted inside. While too many vintage pubs in the city have been stripped of their once-striking interiors, plenty of examples remain of the Victorian legacy of brass taps, stained glass windows, mahogany partitions, and marble counters.

Few are as beautiful as The Swan Bar, owned by the Lynch family, in the center of the city. The existing building dates from 1897, but one inn or another has operated on the corner of York and Aungier Streets since 1739. From its marble bar and its mosaic floor to the bullet holes in its façade that date to the civil war in the 1920s, The Swan is a monument to the history of Ireland. There is an electric bell in the still meticulously-maintained snug, used by generations of women to summon the barkeep, who would send a pint from the bar through drawers that opened on both sides of the exchange.

The Swan Bar has been in the Lynch family since the 1930s. Framed rugby shirts on the walls are a nod to Sean Lynch's career as a rugby player and a framed photograph of him and his teammates, The Lions of '71, dominates one wall.

The pubs of Dublin figure as much in the literary and political imagination of Ireland as in its architectural history. In many of them, including The Brazen Head, the oldest pub in Dublin, Wolfe Tone, Michael Collins, Charles Stewart Parnell, and other nationalists plotted against the English occupation of Ireland.

A preservation order saved The Brazen Head, on Lower Bridge Street, from the scourge of modernity. Although the present building was erected in the 1750s, architectural historians trace innkeeping on that site on the River Liffey back to 1198. Robert Emmet of the United Irishmen kept a room above the front door, the better to watch the comings and goings of the authorities. A sheltering pub could not save him, though: he was captured and executed by the British in 1803.

THE SWAN BAR
Dublin City

Previous spread: The Waxie Dargle, Dublin City. Right and following two spreads: The Swan, with its gorgeous woodwork, gleaming marble, and taps is a slice of history in the heart of Ireland's capital city.

In doggerel and stout let me honor this country though the air is so soft that it smudges the words.

Louis MacNeice

For sheer opulence in a Victorian pub, it is hard to

beat The Stag's Head on Dame Court. Built in 1770, the place is a mélange of marble, mahogany, bottled glass, brass fixtures, and glistening chandeliers. It has counted among its clientele such literary luminaries as James Joyce, the writer driven into exile by the contempt of his countrymen, now embraced by a later generation of Irishmen as a national icon.

Joyce, more than any single Irish writer, is responsible for elevating the simple drinking establishment to near-spiritual importance in the national identity. Jonathan Swift had a decidedly different view, once declaring that "No men in Dublin go to taverns who are worth sitting with." That would be a lot of men. As Leopold Bloom observed in Joyce's famous novel, *Ulysses*: "A good puzzle would be to cross Dublin without passing a pub." Every June 16, Dubliners and tourists alike try to do so, without success. On that day, loyal Joyce readers celebrate "Bloomsday," a celebra-

tion of the date in 1904 described in *Ulysses*, when Bloom and his young companion Stephen Daedelus made their way around the city. Joyce, who lived most of his life on the Continent, once boasted that he could re-create the streets and shops of Dublin from memory.

Davy Byrne's, the pub called the "moral" in *Ulysses* because it did not allow gambling on the premises, was modernized a year before Joyce died in 1941. But the kitchen will still serve you a Gorgonzola cheese sandwich with mustard and a glass of burgundy, the meal that Bloom ordered in the novel, on Bloomsday.

At The Palace Bar, where a previous generation of editors is said to have run the *Irish Times* from the back room, it is possible to imagine Flann O'Brien still on his stool, holding a glass in his gloved hand. Once asked why he wore velvet gloves when he drank, the writer is said to have explained, "I swore to my mother on her deathbed that I'd never touch a glass of whiskey."

THE STAG'S HEAD
Dublin City

Right and following two spreads: The Stag's Head is a comfortable spot to sit for lunch, dinner, or drinks. The beautiful stained glass windows lend an air of prestige and history to this famous pub.

In Ireland the inevitable never happens and the unexpected constantly occurs.

Sir John Pentland Mahaffy

In Toner's, you can hear the echo of the sherry-sipping

William Butler Yeats telling the Dublin writer Oliver St. John Gogarty, "Now I have seen a pub. Please take me home." And in John Mulligan's on Poolbeg Street, you can imagine more appreciative drinkers from the Old Theatre Royal who used to frequent the pub, built in 1782 and said to have been decorated last in 1882. At McDaid's, the mind's eye can summon the not-infrequent sight of the pugnacious Brendan Behan challenging a fellow drinker to step outside.

There were no literary pretensions to the men who put John Kavanagh's of Glasnevin on the map of famous Dublin pubs. Kavanagh's is the only pub in Dublin to have been in the same family for more than a hundred years. The pub was opened in 1833 by John O'Neill in a ground floor room of his home on Prospect Square. Just a year before, the adjacent nine acres had been consecrated as Glasnevin Cemetery. When John Kavanagh took over the taps from his father-in-law, local legend has it that the pub became especially popular with gravediggers, who would knock on the wall when they needed a pint to ease their labors. Eugene Kavanagh, the current owner, is committed to preserving the pub as it has looked for more than 170 years; one day, perhaps, one or more of his six children will be behind the bar.

The McCarthy family of Fethard in County Tipperary shares the Kavanagh clan's passion for preservation. Annette Murphy is the fifth generation of the family to run McCarthy's Hotel. But to call McCarthy's a hotel is to wildly understate its role in the community. Established in the 1850s by Richard McCarthy, the hotel originally housed a grocer, a baker, a draper, a restaurant, a pub, a china shop, a hackney service, and an undertaker. A more modest enterprise today, McCarthy's now has only a pub, a restaurant, and an undertaker business.

The pub is still the heart of the place, its unpolished floors in marked contrast to the gleaming mahogany bar. The scuff marks were made not only by the boots of the local horse set that frequents the pub, but even from the horses themselves: a jockey named Paul Carberry is reputed to have ridden right up to the bar to order a pint.

Horses and the trainers and breeders who tend to them are big business in the surrounding countryside. Winners toast their successes and losers drown their sorrows at McCarthy's after all the races and the hunts. Sometimes the locals share space at the bar with spectral guests: the pub is said to be haunted. Regulars are accustomed to the occasional picture falling from a wall, or unexplained knocking at the pub door.

MCCARTHY'S BAR HOTEL
Fethard, County Tipperary

Right and following spread: Colorful taps line the mahogany bar as comfortably worn stools wait for the next patron.

Above: The best pubs of Ireland—and, in fact, most of the pubs depicted herein—have been awarded the James Joyce Pub Award. They proudly display a handsome bronze plaque, with the great author's likeness, and his words, "A good puzzle would be to cross Dublin without passing a pub." Above right: An old mail slot, layered with paint, on the door to Thomas Connolly's, Sligo Town.

TONER'S
Dublin City

Right and following spread: Toner's of Lower Baggot Street, Dublin, is a small, simple, and very pure pub. The high sturdy stools and well-framed bar and partitions seem to provide the framework for pouring perfect pints of Guinness. Plenty of mirrors reflect so many views and angles that every spot is a grand place to sit. Unique, half-round wooden shelves are mounted on walls everywhere. These mini-altars, outlined by tiny brass rails, are the perfect place to rest your precious pint.

**When money's tight and is hard to get
And your horse has also ran.
When all you have is a heap of debt
A pint of plain is your only man.**

Flann O'Brien

Left and above: Currency from around the world is displayed
near gleaming taps in Toner's.

There are no ghosts to speak of at Morrissey's,

on Main Street of Abbeyleix in County Laois, but the pub is even older than McCarthy's. Established by E. J. Morrissey in 1775, it has not been altered architecturally since 1876, when a second story was put on the building. Here, too, the long bar is mahogany, the snugs are cozy, and the atmosphere is reminiscent of an earlier era. The barman wears a white coat in homage to the pub's earliest incarnation as a grocery shop and an old messenger bicycle hangs on a nicotine-colored wall.

Morrissey's is another favorite watering hole of the local equestrian crowd, who can be found warming themselves on a fall afternoon in front of the wood-burning stove. But the pub's unadulterated interior also attracts a regular stream of tourists traveling the Cork to Dublin road, eager to stop and enjoy a pint of Guinness or a pot of tea and a toasted sandwich in one of the most storied pubs in Ireland.

Whether in the city or the countryside, it will fall to the next generation to determine whether Ireland's traditional pubs are preserved as a refuge from a noisy, homogenized world, where passive entertainment has displaced lively conversation, and canned music from jukeboxes has drowned out the live sounds of fiddles and tin whistles.

Back at Leonard's in Lahardaun, in the shadow of Nephin Mountain, sixteen-year-old Aileen Leonard pours Johnny McAndrew another hot whiskey as Bubbles the sheepdog scampers at her feet. Where would he be this morning if Leonard's were not here, he is asked. "Not here?" he replies. "Why, it's Saturday, isn't it? I am always here on Saturdays."

MORRISSEY'S
Abbeyleix, County Laois

Previous spread: Students from the city music college enjoy a traditional session at The Lobby Pub in Cork City. Right and following spread: Faded Guinness signs and old tins share space with bottles of beer in Morrissey's.